A SLIGHT ACHE

A Play in One Act

by Harold Pinter

samuelfrench.co.uk

FOR AMATEUR PRODUCTION ENQUIRIES

UNITED KINGDOM AND WORLD
EXCLUDING NORTH AMERICA
plays@samuelfrench.co.uk
020 7255 4302/01

Each title is subject to availability from Samuel French,
depending upon country of performance.

THINKING ABOUT PERFORMING A SHOW?

There are thousands of plays and musicals available to perform from Samuel French right now, and applying for a licence is easier and more affordable than you might think

From classic plays to brand new musicals, from monologues to epic dramas, there are shows for everyone.

Plays and musicals are protected by copyright law, so if you want to perform them, the first thing you'll need is a licence. This simple process helps support the playwright by ensuring they get paid for their work and means that you'll have the documents you need to stage the show in public.

Not all our shows are available to perform all the time, so it's important to check and apply for a licence before you start rehearsals or commit to doing the show.

LEARN MORE & FIND THOUSANDS OF SHOWS

Browse our full range of plays and musicals, and find out more about how to license a show
www.samuelfrench.co.uk/perform

Talk to the friendly experts in our Licensing team for advice on choosing a show and help with licensing
plays@samuelfrench.co.uk   020 7387 9373

Acting Editions

BORN TO PERFORM

Playscripts designed from the ground up to work the way you do in rehearsal, performance and study

---

Larger, clearer text for easier reading

Wider margins for notes

Performance features such as character and props lists, sound and lighting cues, and more

---

+ CHOOSE A SIZE AND STYLE TO SUIT YOU

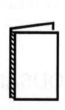

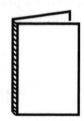

STANDARD EDITION

Our regular paperback book at our regular size

SPIRAL-BOUND EDITION

The same size as the Standard Edition, but with a sturdy, easy-to-fold, easy-to-hold spiral-bound spine

LARGE EDITION

A4 size and spiral bound, with larger text and a blank page for notes opposite every page of text – perfect for technical and directing use

---

LEARN MORE | **samuelfrench.co.uk/actingeditions**

**Other plays by HAROLD PINTER
published and licensed by Samuel French**

Celebration

The Birthday Party

The Caretaker

The Collection

The Dumb Waiter

Family Voices (from the collection *Other Places*)

The Homecoming

A Kind of Alaska (from the collection *Other Places*)

The Lover

Mixed Doubles

Mountain Language

A Night Out

One for the Road (from the collection *Other Places*)

One to Another

The Room

Victoria Station (from the collection *Other Places*)

Other plays by HAROLD PINTER
licensed by Samuel French

Apart from That

Ashes to Ashes

The Basement

Betrayal

The Black and White

The Dwarfs

The Hothouse

Landscape

Last To Go

Monologue

Moonlight

The New World Order

Night School

No Man's Land

Old Times

Party Time

Precisely

Press Conference

FIND PERFECT PLAYS TO PERFORM AT
www.samuelfrench.co.uk/perform

ABOUT THE AUTHOR

Harold Pinter was born in London in 1930. He lived with Antonia Fraser from 1975 until his death on Christmas Eve 2008. (They were married in 1980).

After studying at the Royal Academy of Dramatic Art and the Central School of Speech and Drama, he worked as an actor under the stage name David Baron. Following his success as a playwright, he continued to act under his own name, on stage and screen. He last acted in 2006 when he appeared in Beckett's *Krapp's Last Tape* at the Royal Court Theatre, directed by Ian Rickson.

He wrote twenty-nine plays including *The Birthday Party, The Dumb Waiter, A Slight Ache, The Hothouse, The Caretaker, The Collection, The Lover, The Homecoming, Old Times, No Man's Land, Betrayal, A Kind of Alaska, One For The Road, The New World Order, Moonlight* and *Ashes to Ashes.* Sketches include *The Black and White, Request Stop, That's your Trouble, Night, Precisely, Apart From that* and the recently rediscovered, *Umbrellas.*

He directed twenty-seven theatre productions, including James Joyce's *Exiles*, David Mamet's *Oleanna*, seven plays by Simon Gray (one of which was *Butley* in 1971 which he directed the film of three years later) and many of his own plays including his last, *Celebration*, paired with his first, *The Room* at The Almeida Theatre, London in the spring of 2000.

He wrote twenty-one screenplays including *The Pumpkin Eater, The Servant, The Go-Between, The French Lieutenant's Woman* and *Sleuth.*

In 2005 he received the Nobel Prize for Literature. Other awards include the Companion of Honour for services to Literature, the Legion D'Honneur, the European Theatre Prize the Laurence Olivier Award and the Moliere D'Honneur for lifetime achievement. In 1999 he was made a Companion of Literature by the Royal Society of Literature. Harold Pinter was awarded eighteen honorary degrees.

CHARACTERS

(in the order of their appearance)

FLORA
EDWARD, her husband
THE MATCHSELLER

The action of the Play passes in Flora's and Edward's home on a day in summer

Time – the present

SCENE – **FLORA**'s *and* **EDWARD**'s *home on a day in summer.*

A rostrum across the back has a wide opening leading to a terrace and the garden beyond. Various rooms of the house are indicated. The scullery or kitchen is represented by a folding flat right, with a window in it, though which can be seen the back gate to the garden. The breakfast-room is centre, with a table centre that has upright chairs right and left of it, and a small table up right centre with a bowl of flowers. The study is left, where there is a set of bookshelves. Each section is lit or blacked-out as the action moves from room to room.

When the curtain rises, the lights come up on the breakfast-room centre and the garden area up centre. The table is set for breakfast. **FLORA** *is seated left of the table.* **EDWARD** *is seated right of the table, reading the* "Daily Telegraph". **FLORA** *pours a cup of tea for herself.*

FLORA Have you noticed the honeysuckle this morning?

EDWARD The what?

FLORA The honeysuckle.

EDWARD Honeysuckle? Where?

FLORA By the back gate, Edward.

EDWARD Is that honeysuckle? *(He lowers his paper)* I thought it was - convolvulus, or something.

FLORA But you know it's honeysuckle.

EDWARD I tell you I thought it was convolvulus.

There is a pause.

FLORA It's in wonderful flower.

EDWARD I must look.

FLORA The whole garden's in flower this morning. The clematis. The convolvulus. Everything. I was out at seven. I stood by the pool.

EDWARD Did you say – that the convolvulus was in flower?

FLORA Yes.

EDWARD But good God, you just denied there was any.

FLORA I was talking about the honeysuckle.

EDWARD About the what?

FLORA *(calmly)* Edward – you know that shrub outside the toolshed—

EDWARD Yes, yes.

FLORA —that's convolvulus.

EDWARD That?

FLORA Yes.

EDWARD Oh.

> *There is a pause.*

EDWARD I thought it was japonica.

FLORA Oh, good Lord, no.

EDWARD Pass the teapot, please.

> *There is a pause.* **FLORA** *pours a cup of tea for* **EDWARD** *and adds milk.*

> I don't see why I should be expected to distinguish between these plants. It's not my job.

FLORA You know perfectly well what grows in your garden.

EDWARD Quite the contrary. It is clear that I don't.

There is a pause. **FLORA** *looks at* **EDWARD,** *rises and moves up left centre on to the rostrum.*

FLORA I was up at seven. I stood by the pool. The peace. And everything in flower. The sun was up. You should work in the garden this morning. We could put up the canopy.

EDWARD The canopy? What for?

FLORA To shade you from the sun.

EDWARD Is there a breeze?

FLORA A slight one.

EDWARD It's very treacherous weather, you know.

There is a pause. **FLORA** *faces up stage.*

FLORA Do you know what today is?

EDWARD *(consulting the date on the top of his paper)* Saturday.

FLORA It's the longest day of the year.

EDWARD Really?

FLORA It's the height of summer today.

There is a pause. **EDWARD** *apparently sees a wasp. He puts his paper on the table, rises and stands above his chair.* **FLORA** *turns and moves above her chair left of the table.*

EDWARD Cover the marmalade.

FLORA What?

EDWARD Cover the pot. There's a wasp. Look. Don't move. Keep still.

FLORA *picks up the lid of the marmalade pot.*

What are you doing?

FLORA Covering the pot.

EDWARD Don't move. Leave it. Keep still. Give me the *Telegraph*.

FLORA *hands the paper to* **EDWARD**.

FLORA Don't hit it. It'll bite.

EDWARD Bite? What do you mean – bite? Keep still.

There is a pause.

It's landing.

FLORA It's going in the pot.

EDWARD *(putting the paper on the table)* Give me the lid.

FLORA It's in.

EDWARD Give me the lid.

FLORA I'll do it.

EDWARD Give it to me.

FLORA *hands the lid to* **EDWARD**.

Now – slowly...

FLORA What are you doing?

EDWARD Sh, sh, sh! Slowly...carefully...on...the...pot. *(He puts the lid on the pot)* Very good. *(He resumes his seat)*

FLORA Now he's in the marmalade.

EDWARD Precisely.

There is a pause. **FLORA** *picks up the newspaper then sits left of the table.* **EDWARD** *clenches his eyes, sips his tea.*

FLORA Can you hear him?

EDWARD Hear him?

FLORA Buzzing.

EDWARD Oh, nonsense! How can you hear him? It's an earthenware lid.

FLORA He's becoming frantic.

EDWARD Rubbish! *(He listens for a moment)* Take it away from the table.

FLORA What shall I do with it?

EDWARD Put it in the sink and drown it.

FLORA It'll fly out and bite me.

EDWARD It will not bite you! Wasps don't bite. *(He clenches his eyes)* Anyway, it won't fly out. It's stuck. It'll drown where it is, in the marmalade.

FLORA What a horrible death.

EDWARD On the contrary.

There is a pause. EDWARD *clenches his eyes.*

FLORA Have you got something in your eyes?

EDWARD No. Why do you ask?

FLORA You keep clenching them...blinking them.

EDWARD I have a slight ache in them.

FLORA Oh, dear! *(She faces left and reads the paper)*

EDWARD Yes. A slight ache. As if I hadn't slept.

FLORA Did you sleep, Edward?

EDWARD Of course I slept. Uninterrupted. As always.

FLORA And yet you feel tired.

EDWARD I didn't say I felt tired. I merely said I had a slight ache in my eyes.

FLORA *(turning)* Why is that, then? *(She lowers the paper)*

EDWARD I really don't know.

There is a pause.

FLORA Oh, goodness! *(She folds up the paper)*

EDWARD What is it?

FLORA I can see it. It's trying to come out.

EDWARD How can it?

FLORA Through the hole. It's trying to crawl out – through the spoon hole.

EDWARD Mmm – yes. *(He half rises)* Can't do it, of course. *(He pauses then resumes his seat)* Oh, let's kill it, for goodness' sake!

FLORA Yes, let's. But how?

EDWARD *(after a pause)* Bring it out on the spoon and squash it on a plate.

FLORA It'll fly away. It'll bite.

EDWARD If you don't stop using that word I shall leave the table.

FLORA *(after a pause)* But wasps do bite.

EDWARD They don't bite. They sting. It's snakes – that bite.

FLORA *(after a pause)* What about horseflies?

EDWARD *(after a pause)* Horseflies suck.

There is a pause.

FLORA *(tentatively)* If we – if we wait long enough, I suppose it'll choke to death. It'll suffocate in the marmalade.

EDWARD *(briskly)* You do know I've got work to do this morning, don't you? I can't spend the whole day worrying about a wasp.

FLORA Well – kill it.

EDWARD You want to kill it?

FLORA Yes.

EDWARD Very well. Pass me the hot-water jug.

FLORA What are you going to do?

EDWARD Scald it. *(He rises)*

There is a pause.

(he picks up the hot-water jug) Now...

FLORA *(whispering)* Do you want me to lift the lid?

EDWARD No, no, no. I'll pour down the spoon hole. Right –
down the spoon hole.

FLORA Listen!

EDWARD What?

FLORA It's buzzing.

EDWARD *bends over the pot and listens.*

EDWARD *(straightening up)* Vicious creatures. *(He pauses)*
Curious, but I don't remember seeing any wasps at all, all
summer, until now. I'm sure I don't know why. I mean –
there must have been wasps.

FLORA Please.

EDWARD This couldn't be the first wasp, could it?

FLORA Please.

EDWARD The first wasp of summer? No. It's not possible.

FLORA Edward.

EDWARD Mmmmm?

FLORA Kill it.

EDWARD Ah, yes. Tilt the pot. Tilt.

FLORA *tilts the pot.*

Aah— Down here— *(He pours)* Right down— Blinding
him— *(He puts the jug on the table)* That's it. *(He rubs his
hands together and resumes his seat)*

FLORA Is it?

EDWARD Lift the lid.

> **FLORA** *hesitates.*

> All right, I will. *(He removes the lid from the pot and puts it on the table)* There he is. *(He takes the wasp from the pot with the spoon)* Dead. What a monster. *(He squashes the wasp on his plate, rises and moves up right centre on to the rostrum)*

FLORA What an awful experience. *(She reads the paper)*

EDWARD What a beautiful day it is. Beautiful. *(He breathes deeply three times, then coughs)* I think I shall work in the garden this morning. Where's that canopy?

FLORA It's in the shed.

EDWARD Yes, we must get it out. My goodness, just look at that sky. Not a cloud. Did you say it was the longest day of the year today?

FLORA Yes.

EDWARD Ah, it's a good day. I feel it in my bones. In my muscles. I think I'll stretch my legs in a minute. Down to the pool. *(He exercises)* My God, look at that flowering shrub over there.

> **FLORA** *is pleased.*

> *(after a pause)* Clematis.

> **FLORA** *ceases to be pleased.*

> *(he looks off right)* What a wonderful... *(He stops suddenly)*

FLORA What?

> *There is a pause.*

> *(she turns to face him)* Edward. What is it?

> *There is a pause.*

> Edward...

EDWARD *(turning to* FLORA*)* He's there.

FLORA Who?

EDWARD Blast and damn it, he's there, he's there at the back gate.

FLORA Let me see. *(She rises, puts the paper on her chair and moves to left of* EDWARD. *Lightly)* Oh, it's the matchseller.

EDWARD He's back again.

FLORA But he's always there.

EDWARD Why? What is he doing there?

FLORA *(moving above the table)* But he's never disturbed you, has he? *(She takes a cigarette and a cigarette holder from the box on the table)* The man's been standing there for weeks. *(She puts the cigarette in the holder)* You've never mentioned it.

EDWARD What is he doing there?

There is a pause. EDWARD *moves down right centre, then crosses down left.*

FLORA He's selling matches, of course.

EDWARD It's ridiculous. What's the time?

FLORA Half past nine.

EDWARD What in God's name is he doing with a tray full of matches at half past nine in the morning?

FLORA He arrives at seven o'clock.

EDWARD *(turning to* FLORA*)* Seven o'clock?

FLORA He's always there at seven.

EDWARD Yes, but you've never – actually seen him arrive?

FLORA No, I...

EDWARD Well, how do you know he's – not been standing there all night? *(He turns away)*

FLORA *(after a pause)* Do you find him interesting, Edward?

EDWARD *(casually)* Interesting? No. No, I...don't find him interesting.

FLORA He's a very nice old man, really.

EDWARD You've spoken to him?

FLORA No. No, I haven't spoken to him. *(She lights her cigarette)* I've nodded.

EDWARD *(pacing to right centre)* For two months he's been standing on that spot, do you realize that? *(He turns and paces to left)* Two months. I haven't been able to step outside the back gate.

FLORA Why on earth not?

EDWARD *(to himself)* It used to give me great pleasure, such pleasure, to stroll along through the long grass, out through the back gate, pass into the lane. That pleasure is now denied me. It's my own house, isn't it? *(He faces front)* It's my own gate.

FLORA I really can't understand this, Edward.

EDWARD Damn! And do you know I've never seen him sell one box? Not a box. It's hardly surprising. He's on the wrong road. It's not a road at all. What is it? It's a lane, leading to a monastery. Off everybody's route. Even the monks take a short cut. No one goes up it. Why doesn't he stand on the main road if he wants to sell matches, by the *front* gate? The whole thing's preposterous.

FLORA I don't know why you're getting so excited about it. He's a quiet, harmless old man, going about his business. He's quite harmless.

EDWARD *(crossing to right centre)* I didn't say he wasn't harmless. Of course he's harmless. How could he be other than harmless?

The lights dim to blackout. During the blackout, FLORA
*exits up right. The table and chairs centre are removed.
Two armchairs are set left centre and left. A wicker
armchair is set centre of the terrace. A canopy or awning
is set over the terrace.*

*The lights come up on the terrace and on the kitchen
area right.* EDWARD *is standing at the kitchen window
gazing out.*

FLORA *(off up right)* Edward, where are you? Edward? Where
are you, Edward? *(Nearer)* Edward?

FLORA *enters up right and moves to left of* EDWARD.

Edward, what are you doing in the scullery?

EDWARD Doing?

FLORA I've been looking everywhere for you. I put up the canopy
ages ago. I came back and you were nowhere to be seen.
Have you been out?

EDWARD No.

FLORA Where have you been?

EDWARD Here.

FLORA I looked in your study. I even went into the attic.

EDWARD *(tonelessly)* What would I be doing in the attic?

FLORA *(after a pause)* I couldn't imagine what had happened
to you. Do you know it's twelve o'clock.

EDWARD Is it?

FLORA I even went to the bottom of the garden to see if you
were in the toolshed.

EDWARD *(tonelessly)* What would I be doing in the toolshed?

FLORA You must have seen me in the garden. You can see
through the window.

EDWARD Only part of the garden.

FLORA Yes, but...

EDWARD Only a corner of the garden. *(He pauses)* A very small corner.

FLORA *(with a step towards him)* What are you doing in here?

EDWARD Nothing. *(He pauses)* I was digging out some notes, that's all.

FLORA Notes?

EDWARD For my essay.

FLORA Which essay?

EDWARD My essay on space and time.

FLORA I don't know that one.

EDWARD You don't know it?

FLORA I thought you were writing one about the Belgian Congo.

EDWARD I've been engaged on the dimensionality and continuity of space – and time – for years.

FLORA And the Belgian Congo?

EDWARD *(shortly)* Never mind about the Belgian Congo.

There is a pause.

FLORA *(with a step towards him)* But you don't keep notes in the scullery. *(She turns to the window)*

EDWARD You'd be surprised. You'd be highly surprised.

FLORA *(gazing out of the window)* Good Lord, what's that. Is that a bullock let loose? No. It's the matchseller. My goodness, you can see him – through the hedge. He looks much bigger from here. Have you been watching him? He looks – like a bullock. *(She pauses then turns to him)* Edward, are you coming outside? I've put up the canopy. You'll miss the best of the day. You can have an hour before lunch.

EDWARD I've no work to do this morning.

FLORA What about your essay? *(She moves to right of* EDWARD*)* You don't intend to stay in the scullery all day, do you?

EDWARD Get out. Leave me alone.

FLORA *(after a slight pause)* You've never spoken to me like that in all your life.

EDWARD Yes, I have.

FLORA Oh, Weddie. Beddie-Weddie...

EDWARD *(turning to face her)* Do not call me that!

FLORA Your eyes are bloodshot.

EDWARD *(looking away)* Damn it!

FLORA It's too dark in here to peer...

EDWARD Damn!

FLORA It's so bright outside.

EDWARD Damn!

FLORA And it's dark in here.

EDWARD Damn!

FLORA *(after a pause)* You're frightened of him.

EDWARD I'm not.

FLORA You're frightened of a poor old man. Why?

EDWARD I am not!

FLORA He's a poor, harmless old man.

EDWARD It's my eyes. *(He puts his hands over his eyes)*

FLORA Let me bathe them.

EDWARD Keep away. *(He pauses. Slowly)* I want to speak to that man. I want to have a word with him. *(He pauses and crosses below* FLORA *to right)* It's quite absurd, of course. I really can't tolerate something so – absurd right on my doorstep. I shall not tolerate it. He hasn't sold one match all morning. No one passed. Yes. A monk passed. A non-smoker. In a loose garment. It's quite obvious he was a non-smoker, but still, the man made no effort. He made no effort to clinch a sale, to rid himself of one of his cursed boxes. His one chance, all morning, and he made no effort. *(He pauses)* I haven't wasted my time. I've hit, in fact, upon the truth. He's not a matchseller at all. The bastard isn't a matchseller at all. Curious I never realized that before. He's an impostor. *(He takes a step towards* FLORA*)* I watched him very closely. He made no move towards the monk. As for the monk – the monk made no move towards him. The monk was moving along the lane. He didn't pause, or halt, or in any way alter his step. As for the matchseller – how ridiculous to go on calling him by that title. What a farce. No, there is something very false about that man. I intend to get to the bottom of it. I'll soon get rid of him. He can go and ply his trade somewhere else. Instead of standing like a bullock – a bullock, outside my back gate.

FLORA But if he isn't a matchseller, what is his trade?

EDWARD *(crossing to centre)* We'll soon find out.

FLORA You're going out to speak to him?

EDWARD *(turning to her)* Certainly not! Go out to *him?* Certainly – not. I'll invite him in here. Into my study. Then we'll get to the bottom of it.

FLORA Why don't you call the police and have him removed? *(She pauses then takes a step towards* EDWARD*)* Why don't you call the police, Edward? You could say he was a public nuisance. Although I... I can't say I find him a nuisance.

EDWARD Call him in.

FLORA Me?

EDWARD Go out and call him in.

FLORA Are you serious? *(She pauses)* Edward, I could call the police.

EDWARD *moves left centre.*

Or even the vicar.

EDWARD Go and get him.

> FLORA *moves up centre on to the rostrum. The lights
> on the kitchen area dim to blackout.* EDWARD *crosses
> to the bookshelves left, takes a cigarette from the box
> on it, lights the cigarette then sits in the armchair left.*

> *The* MATCHSELLER *enters up right and stands by the
> back gate. He wears a balaclava and carries a pedlar's
> tray with boxes of matches.*

FLORA *(looking off right)* Good morning. *(She pauses)* We
haven't met. I live in this house here. My husband and I.
(She pauses) I wonder if you could... Would you care for a
cup of tea? *(She pauses)* Or a glass of lemon? It must be
so dry standing there. *(She pauses and takes a step or two
right)* Might I buy your tray of matches, do you think? We've
run out completely, and we always keep a very large stock.
It happens that way, doesn't it? *(She pauses and moves to
the gate)* Come and have lunch with us. This way, that's
right. May I take your arm? *(She takes the* MATCHSELLER*'s
arm)* This way.

> FLORA *and the* MATCHSELLER *move along the rostrum
> to left centre.*

Mind now. Isn't it beautiful weather? It's the longest day of
the year, today. That's honeysuckle. And there's convolvulus.
There's clematis. And you see that plant by the conservatory?
That's japonica.

> *The lights come up on the study left.*

(she moves to EDWARD*)* He's here.

EDWARD I know.

FLORA He's in the hall.

EDWARD I know he's here. I can smell him.

FLORA Smell him?

EDWARD Can't you smell the house now?

FLORA What are you going to do with him, Edward? You won't be rough with him in any way? He's very old. I'm not sure if he can hear, or even see. And he's wearing the oldest...

EDWARD I don't want to know what he's wearing.

FLORA But you'll see for yourself in a minute, if you speak to him.

EDWARD I shall.

FLORA (after a slight pause) He's an old man.

EDWARD looks quickly at FLORA, then away.

You won't – be rough with him?

EDWARD If he's so old, why doesn't he seek shelter – from the storm?

FLORA But there's no storm. It's summer, the longest day...

EDWARD There was a storm, last week. A summer storm. He stood without moving, while it thundered all round him.

FLORA When was this?

EDWARD He remained quite still, while the wind raged round him.

There is a pause.

FLORA Edward – are you sure it's wise to bother about all this?

EDWARD Tell him to come in.

FLORA I...

EDWARD Now.

FLORA moves to left of the MATCHSELLER.

FLORA. Hullo. Would you like to go in? *(She pauses)* You can have some sherry before lunch.

The **MATCHSELLER** *moves a little down left centre.*

That's right. This way. I'll join you – later.

FLORA *exits up left.*

EDWARD Don't stand out there, old chap. Come into my study. *(He rises, humming to himself, and crosses to right centre)* Come in. That's right.

The **MATCHSELLER** *moves down left centre and trips slightly.*

Mind how you go. That's – it.

The **MATCHSELLER** *stands left of the chair left centre.*

Now. Make yourself comfortable. Thought you might like some refreshment on a day like this. Sit down, old man. What will you have? Sherry? Or what about a double whisky? Eh? *(He pauses)* I entertain the villagers annually, as a matter of fact. I'm not the squire, but they look upon me with some regard. Don't believe we've got a squire here anymore, actually. Don't know what became of him. Nice old man, he was. Great chess player, as I remember. Three daughters. The pride of the county. Flaming red hair. Alice was the eldest. Sit yourself down, old chap. Eunice I think was number two. The youngest one was the pick of the bunch. Sally. No, no, wait a minute, no, it wasn't Sally, it was – Fanny. Fanny. A flower. *(He pauses)* You must be a stranger here. Unless you lived here once, went on a long voyage and have lately returned. Do you know the district? *(He pauses)* Now, now, you mustn't...stand about like that. Take a seat. Which one would you prefer? We have a great variety. Can't stand uniformity. Like different seats, different backs. Often when I'm working, you know, I draw up one chair, scribble a few lines, put it by, draw up another, sit back, ponder, put it by— *(He clenches his eyes)* sit back – put it by... *(He pauses)*

I write theological and philosophical essays. *(He pauses)*
Now and again I jot down a few observations on certain
tropical phenomena – not from the same standpoint, of
course. *(He pauses)* Yes. Africa, now. Africa's always been my
happy hunting ground. Fascinating country. Do you know
it? I get the impression that you've – been around a bit. Do
you by any chance know the Membunza Mountains? Great
range south of Katambaloo. French Equatorial Africa, if my
memory serves me right. Most extraordinary diversity of
flora and fauna. Especially fauna. I understand in the Gobi
Desert you can come across some very strange sights. Never
been there myself. Studied the maps, though. Fascinating
things, maps. *(He pauses)* Sit down. *(He pauses)* I say, can
you hear me? *(He pauses)* I said— "I say, can you hear me?"
(He pauses) You possess most extraordinary repose, for a
man of your age, don't you? Well, perhaps that's not quite the
right word...repose. Do you find it chilly in here? *(He moves
up centre to the edge of the rostrum)* I'm sure it's chillier in
here than out. I haven't been out yet, today, though I shall
probably spend the whole afternoon working, in the garden,
under my canopy, at my table by the pool. Oh, I understand
you met my *wife.* *(He moves down centre)* Charming woman,
don't you think? *(He moves right centre)* Plenty of grit there,
too. Stood by me through thick and thin, that woman. In
season and out of season. Fine figure of a woman she was,
too, in her youth. Wonderful carriage, flaming red hair...
(He stops abruptly. After a pause) Yes, I... I was in much the
same position myself, then, as you are now, you understand?
Struggling to make my way in the world. I was in commerce,
too. *(With a chuckle)* Oh, yes, I know what it's like - the
weather, the rain, beaten from pillar to post, up hill and
down dale - the rewards were few - winters in hovels -
up till all hours, working at your thesis - yes, I've done it
all. *(He pauses)* Let me advise you. Get a good woman to
stick by you. Never mind what the world says. Keep at it.
Keep your shoulder to the wheel. It'll pay dividends. *(He
pauses, realizes his cigarette ash is long, crosses and uses
the ashtray on the bookshelves left. With a laugh)* You must

excuse my chatting away like this. *(He moves to the chair left centre and sits)* We have few visitors this time of the year. All our friends summer abroad. I'm a home bird myself. Wouldn't mind taking a trip to Asia Minor, mind you, or to certain lower regions of the Congo, but Europe? Out of the question. Much too noisy. I'm sure you agree. Now, look, what will you have to drink? A glass of ale? Curaçao? Ginger beer? Tia Maria? A Wachenheimer Fuchsmantel Riesling Beeren Auslese? Gin and It? Châteauneuf-du-Pape? A little Asti Spumante? Or what do you say to a straightforward Piesporter Goldtropfschen Feine Auslese Reichs-graf von Kesselstaff? Any preference? *(He pauses)* You look a trifle warm. Why don't you take off your balaclava? I'd find that a little itchy myself. But then I've always been one for freedom of movement. Even in the depth of winter I wear next to nothing. *(He stretches)* I don't want to seem inquisitive but aren't you rather on the wrong road for matchselling? Not terribly busy, is it? Of course you may not care for petrol fumes, or the noise of traffic. I can quite understand that. *(He pauses)* Do forgive me peering, but is that a glass eye you're wearing? *(He pauses)* Do take off your balaclava, there's a good chap. Put your tray down and take your ease, as they say in this part of the world. *(He crosses to the MATCHSELLER)* I must say you keep quite a good stock, don't you? Tell me, between ourselves, are those boxes full, or are there just a few half empty ones among them? Oh, yes, I used to be in commerce. *(He crosses to right and turns)*

The MATCHSELLER *trembles.*

Look out! Mind your tray!

The MATCHSELLER *drops his tray and the matchboxes spill.*

Good God, what...? *(He pauses)* You've dropped your... *(He crosses, kneels, collects all but two boxes and puts them on the tray)* Eh, these boxes are all wet. You've no right to sell wet matches, you know. *(He grunts)* Uuuuuugggh. This feels suspiciously like fungus. You won't get far in this trade if you don't take care of your goods. *(He realizes he is kneeling at the* MATCHSELLER'S *feet. He puts the remaining two boxes on the tray, rises, moves to left of the* MATCHSELLER *and holds out the tray)* Here's your tray.

The MATCHSELLER *takes the tray with his right hand. His left hand slowly closes in on the tray.*

(He sits in the chair left centre and brushes the dust from his knees) Now listen, let me be quite frank with you, shall I? I really cannot understand why you don't sit down. I can't possibly talk to you unless you're settled. Then and only then can I speak to you. Do you follow me? You're not being terribly helpful. *(He pauses)* You're sweating. The sweat's pouring out of you. Take off that balaclava. *(He pauses)* Go into the corner, then. Into the shade of the corner. Go on. *(He pauses)* Get back. *(He pauses then smacks his knee)* Back.

The MATCHSELLER *moves centre.*

Back. Back.

The MATCHSELLER *moves right.*

Ah, you understand me. Forgive me for saying so, but I had decided that you had the comprehension of a bullock. I was mistaken. You understand me perfectly well. Now I can get down to brass tacks. Can't I? *(He pauses)* No doubt you're wondering why I invited you into this house? You may think I was alarmed by the look of you. You would be quite mistaken. I was not alarmed by the look of you. I did not find you at all alarming. No, no. Nothing outside this room has ever alarmed me. *(He pauses)* You disgusted me, quite forcibly, if you want to know the truth. *(He pauses)* Why did you disgust me to that extent? That seems to be a pertinent question. You're no more disgusting than Fanny, the squire's daughter, after all. In appearance you differ but not in essence. There's the same— *(He pauses)* the same... *(He pauses. In a low voice)* I want to ask you a question.

Why do you stand outside my back gate, from dawn till dusk? Why do you pretend to sell matches?

The **MATCHSELLER** *begins to tremble.*

Why? Come here. *(He rises)*

The **MATCHSELLER** *moves to the chair left centre.*

Come here. Mind your tray. *(He moves above the chair left centre)* Come, quick, quick. Sit here.

The **MATCHSELLER** *crosses to the chair left.*

Sit – sit in this. No, no, not there. No!

The **MATCHSELLER** *slowly sits in the chair left.*

Aaaah! You've sat. At last. What a relief. *(He pauses)* My chair comfortable? I bought it in a sale. I bought all the furniture in this house in a sale. The same sale. When I was a young man, You, too, perhaps. *(He pauses)* You, too, perhaps. *(He pauses)* At the same time, perhaps. *(He calls)* Flora!

FLORA *(offstage; calling)* Yes?

EDWARD I must get some air. *(He moves up left centre on to the rostrum)*

FLORA enters up left.

Flora! I must get a breath of air.

The lights fade on the study left.

FLORA Come under the canopy.

EDWARD Ah! *(He sits in the wicker chair up centre on the rostrum)* The peace. The peace out here.

FLORA Look at your trees.

EDWARD Yes.

FLORA Our own trees. Can you hear the birds?

EDWARD No, I can't hear them.

FLORA *(standing right of* EDWARD*)* But they're singing, high up, and flapping.

EDWARD Good. Let them flap.

FLORA Shall I bring your lunch out here? You can have it in peace, and a quiet drink, under your canopy. *(She pauses)* How are you getting on with your old man?

EDWARD What do you mean?

FLORA What's happening? How are you getting on with him?

EDWARD Very well. We get on remarkably well. He's a little... reticent. Somewhat withdrawn. It's understandable. I should be the same, perhaps, in his place. Though, of course, I could not possibly find myself in his place.

FLORA Have you found out anything about him?

EDWARD A little. A little. He's had various trades, that's certain. His place of residence is unsure. He's...he's not a drinking man. I haven't discovered the reason for his arrival here. I shall in due course – by nightfall.

FLORA Is it necessary?

EDWARD Necessary?

FLORA *(quickly)* I could show him out now, it wouldn't matter. You've seen him, he's harmless, unfortunate – old – that's all. *(She perches on the arm of* EDWARD*'s chair and puts her arm around his shoulders)* Edward – listen – he's not here through any...design, or anything, I know it. I mean, he might just as well stand outside our back gate as anywhere else. He'll move on, I can...make him. I promise you. There's no point in upsetting yourself like this. He's an old man, weak in the head...that's all.

EDWARD *(after a pause)* You're deluded.

FLORA *(rising)* Edward...

EDWARD You're deluded. And stop calling me "Edward".

FLORA You're not still frightened of him?

EDWARD Frightened of him? Of *him?* Have you *seen* him? *(He pauses)* He's like jelly. A great bullockfat of jelly. He can't see straight. I think as a matter of fact, he wears a glass eye. He's almost stone deaf. He's very nearly dead on his feet. Why should he frighten me? No, you're a woman, you know nothing. *(He pauses)* But he possesses other faculties. Cunning. The man's an impostor and he knows I know it.

FLORA I'll tell you what. Look. *(She moves down right)* Let me speak to him. I'll speak to him.

EDWARD And I know he knows I know it.

FLORA I'll find out all about him, Edward. I promise you I will.

EDWARD And he knows I know.

FLORA *(moving up centre to the edge of the rostrum)* Edward! Listen to me! I can find out all about him. I promise you. I shall go and have a word with him now. I shall – get to the bottom of it.

EDWARD You?

FLORA You'll see – he won't bargain for me. I'll surprise him. He'll...he'll admit everything.

EDWARD *(rising; softly)* He'll admit everything, will he?

FLORA You wait and see, you just wait and see.

EDWARD *(moving to* **FLORA***; hissing)* What are you plotting?

FLORA I know exactly what I shall do.

EDWARD *(seizing* **FLORA** *by the arms)* What are you plotting?

FLORA You're hurting me!

    EDWARD *releases* **FLORA**.

I shall get to the truth of it, I assure you. You're much too heavy-handed, in every way. You should trust your wife more, Edward. You should trust her judgement, and have a greater insight into her capabilities. A woman...a woman will often succeed, you know, where a man must invariably fail. I shall wave from the window when I am ready, and then you can come in.

EDWARD *exits up left. The lights come up on the study.*

(she moves left centre) Do you mind if I come in? Are you comfortable? *(She pauses)* Oh, the sun's shing directly on you. Wouldn't you rather sit in the shade?

The lights start very slowly to dim.

(she sits in the chair left centre) It's the longest day of the year today, did you know that? Actually the year has flown. I can remember Christmas and that dreadful frost. And the floods. We were out of danger up here, of course, but in the valleys whole families, I remember, drifted away on the current. The country was a lake. Everything stopped. We lived on our own preserves, drank elderberry wine, studied other cultures. *(She pauses)* Do you know, I've a feeling I've seen you before, somewhere. Long before the flood. You were much younger. Yes, I'm really sure of it. Between ourselves, were you ever a poacher? I had an encounter with a poacher once. It was a ghastly rape, the brute. High up on a hillside cattle track. Early spring. I was out riding, on my pony. And there on the verge a man lay – ostensibly injured, lying on his front, I remember, possibly the victim of a murderous assault – how was I to know? I dismounted. I went to him, he rose, I fell, my pony took off, down the valley. I saw the sky through the trees, blue. Up to my ears in mud. It was a desperate battle. *(She pauses)* I lost. *(She pauses)* Of course, life was perilous in those days. It was my first canter unchaperoned. *(She pauses)* Years later, when I was a Justice of Peace for the county, I had him in front of the Bench. He was there for poaching. That's how I know he was a poacher. The evidence though, was sparse, inadmissible. I acquitted him, letting him off with a caution.

He'd grown a red beard, I remember. Yes. A bit of a stinker. *(She pauses)* I say, you are perspiring, aren't you? Shall I mop your brow? With my chiffon? Is it the heat? Or the closeness? Or confined space? Or...? *(She rises and moves to him)* Actually, the day is cooling. It'll soon be dusk. Perhaps it is dusk. May I? *(She mops the MATCHSELLER's brow)* You don't mind? *(She pauses)* Ah, there, that's better. And your cheeks. *(She chuckles)* It's a woman's job, isn't it? And I'm the only woman on hand. There. *(She pauses. Intimately)* Tell me, have you a woman? Do you like women? *(She puts her handkerchief in her pocket)* Do you ever – think about women? *(She pauses)* Have you ever – stopped a woman? *(She backs a step or two)* I'm sure you must have been quite attractive once. *(She moves to the chair left centre)* Not any more, of course. You've got a vile smell. Vile. Quite repellent, in fact. *(She sits)* Sex, I suppose, means nothing to you. I wonder if you realize that sex is a very vital experience for other people? Really, I think you'd amuse me if you weren't so hideous. You're probably quite amusing in your own way. *(Seductively)* Speak to me of love. Tell me all about love. *(She looks at him)* God knows what you're saying. It's quite disgusting. Do you know, when I was a girl I loved...I loved...I simply adored... What *have* you got on, for goodness' sake? A jersey? *(She rises and moves to him)* It's clogged. Have you been rolling in mud? *(She pauses)* You haven't been rolling in mud, have you? And what have you got under your jersey? Let's see. *(She lifts his jersey)* I'm not tickling you, am I? No. Good...Lord, is this a vest? That's quite original. Quite original. Hmmmm, you're a solid old boy, I must say. Not at all like a jelly. *(She perches on the upstage arm of the MATCHSELLER's chair)* All you need is a bath. A lovely lathery bath. And a good scrub. A lovely lathery scrub. *(She pauses)* Don't you? It will be a pleasure. *(She puts her arm around him)* I'm going to keep you. I'm going to keep you, you dreadful chap, and call you "Barnabas". Isn't it dark, Barnabas? Your eyes, your eyes, your great big eyes. *(She rises and backs a step)* My husband would never have guessed your name. Never. *(She kneels at his feet.*

Whispering) It's me you were waiting for, wasn't it? You've been standing waiting for me. You've seen me in the woods, picking daisies, in my apron, my pretty daisy apron, and you came and stood, poor creature, at my gate, till death us do part. Poor Barnabas. I'm going to put you to bed. I'm going to put you to bed and watch over you. But first you must have a good whacking bath. And I'll buy you pretty little things that will suit you. And little toys to play with. On your death-bed. Why shouldn't you die happy?

EDWARD *enters up left and crosses to right of the chair left centre.*

(she rises and stands left of the chair left centre. To **EDWARD***)* Don't come in. He's dying.

The lights continue to slowly dim.

EDWARD Dying. He's not dying.

FLORA I tell you he's very ill.

EDWARD He's not dying. Nowhere near. He'll see you cremated.

FLORA The man is desperately ill.

EDWARD Ill? You lying slut. Get back to your trough.

FLORA Edward...

EDWARD *(violently)* To your trough!

FLORA *exits up left.*

Good evening to you. Why are you sitting in the gloom? Oh, you've begun to disrobe. Take off all your togs, if you like. Make yourself at home. Strip to your buff. Do as you would in your own house. Did you say something? *(Pause)* Did you say something? *(Pause. He sits in the chair left centre)* Well, then, tell me about your boyhood, mmm? *(He pauses)* What did you do with it? Run? Swim? Kick the ball? You kicked the ball? What position? Left back? Goal? First reserve? *(He pauses)* I used to play, myself. Country house matches, mostly. Kept wicket and batted number seven. *(He pauses and clenches his eyes)* Kept wicket and batted number seven. Man called...Cavendish, I think, had something of your style. Bowled left arm over the wicket. Always kept his cap on, quite a dab hand at solo whist, preferred a good round of prop and cop to anything else. On wet days the field was swamped. *(He pauses)* Perhaps you don't play cricket. Perhaps you never met Cavendish and never played cricket. You look less and less like a cricketer the more I see of you. Where did you live in those days? God damn it, I'm entitled to know something about you. You're in my blasted house, on my territory, drinking my wine, eating my duck. Now you've had your fill you sit like a hump, a mouldering heap. In my room. My den. *(He pauses)* I can rem... *(He stops abruptly. After a pause)* You find that funny? Are you grinning? *(He pauses. In disgust)* Is that a grin on your face? *(Further disgust)* It's lopsided. It's all... down on one side. You're grinning. It amuses you, does it? When I tell you how well I remember this room, how well I remember this den. *(He pauses)* Ha! Yesterday now, it was clear, clearly defined, so clearly. *(He pauses)* The garden, too, was sharp, lucid, in the sun, in the rain. *(He pauses)* My den too, was sharp, arranged for my purpose – quite satisfactory. The house, too, was polished, all the banisters were polished, and the stair rods, and the curtain rods. My desk was polished, and my cabinet. I was polished. *(Nostalgic)* I could stand on the hill and look through my telescope at the sea. *(He mimes looking through a telescope)* And follow the path of the three-masted schooner, feeling fit, well aware of my sinews, their suppleness, my arms lifted holding the telescope, steadily, easily no trembling, my aim was perfect. I could pour hot water down the spoon hole, yes, easily, no difficulty, my grasp firm, my command established, my life was accounted for. After my long struggling against all kinds of usurpers, disreputables, lists, literally lists of people anxious to do me down, and my reputation down, my command was established. All summer I would breakfast, survey my landscape – take my telescope, examine the overhanging of the hedges, pursue the narrow lane past the monastery, climb the hill... *(He mimes looking through the telescope)* Adjust the lens, watch the progress of the three-masted schooner, my progress was as sure, as fluent. *(He pauses and slowly drops his arms)* Yes, yes, you're quite right, it is funny. *(He pauses)* Laugh your bloody head off! Go on. Don't mind me. No need to be polite. That's right. *(He pauses)* You're quite right, it is funny. I'll laugh with you. Ha ha ha! Yes! You're laughing with me. I'm laughing with you. We're laughing together. Ha ha ha! *(Brightly)* Why did I invite you into this room? That's your next question, isn't it? Bound to be. *(He pauses)* Well, "Why not?" you might say. My oldest acquaintance. My nearest and dearest. My kith and kin. Ah, that's good for a guffaw, is it? That's good for a belly laugh? Go on, then. Let it out. Let yourself go, for God's... *(He catches his breath)* You're crying. *(He pauses. Moved)* You haven't been laughing. You're crying. *(He pauses)* You're weeping. You're shaking with grief. For me? I can't believe it. For my plight. I've been wrong. *(He pauses. Briskly)* Come, come, stop it. Be a man. Blow your nose, for goodness' sake. Pull yourself together. *(He sneezes)* Ah. *(He sneezes)* Ah. Fever. Excuse me. *(He rises)* I've caught a cold. A germ. In my eyes. It was this morning. In my eyes. *(He slowly collapses to the floor as though in a faint, lies for a moment, then supports himself on his right hand)* Not that I had any difficulty in seeing you. No, no, it was not so much my sight, my sight is excellent – in winter I run about with nothing on but a pair of polo shorts – no, it was not so much any deficiency in my sight as the airs between me and my object – don't weep – the change of air, the currents obtaining in the space between me and my object, the shades they make, the shapes they take, the quivering, the eternal quivering – please stop crying – nothing to do with heat-haze. *(He pauses)* Sometimes, of course, I would take shelter, shelter to compose myself. Yes, I would seek a tree, a cranny of bushes, erect my canopy and so make shelter. *(He lies down)* I lay on my side in my polo shorts, my fingers lightly in contact with the blades of grass, the underside of all the great foliage dark above me. Nothing entered my nook. Nothing left it. *(He curls up like a child. After a short pause, he rises slowly on to his knees)* But then the time came. I saw the wind. I saw the wind swirling, and the dust at my back gate lifting, and the long grass scything together.

The **MATCHSELLER** *stirs.*

(slowly, in horror) You *are* laughing. You're laughing. Your face. Your body. *(Overwhelming nausea and horror)* Rocking, gasping—rocking—shaking—rocking—heaving—rocking... You're laughing at *me!* *(He screams and puts his hands over his ears)*

The **MATCHSELLER** *rises.*

You look younger. You look extraordinarily youthful. *(He pauses)* You want to examine the garden? The plants? Where I run. My track in training - I was number one sprinter - licked men twice my strength - when a stripling - like yourself. *(He pauses)* The pool must be listening in the moonlight. The cliff. The sea. The three-masted... *(With a final effort)* Who are you?

FLORA *(offstage)* Barnabas?

There is a pause.

FLORA *enters up left and moves to right of the chair left centre.*

Ah, Barnabas, everything is ready. I want to show you my garden, your garden. You must see my japonica, my convolvulus - my honeysuckle, my clematis. *(She pauses)* Summer is coming. I've put up the canopy for you. You can lunch in the garden by the pool. I've polished the whole house for you. *(She holds out her right arm)*

The **MATCHSELLER** *moves to* **FLORA***, takes her arm and they move up left centre to the foot of the rostrum.*

There. There. *(She pauses)* Oh, wait a moment. *(She takes the tray from the* **MATCHSELLER***)* Edward. Here is your tray.

FLORA *hands the tray to* **EDWARD,** *moves to left of the* **MATCHSELLER** *and they move into the garden as the lights blackout and—*

The curtain falls.

FURNITURE AND PROPERTY LIST

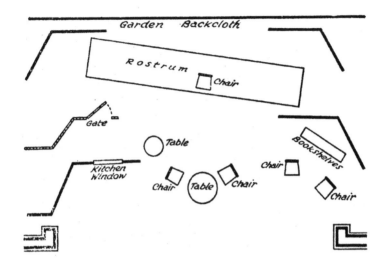

Onstage: Table (centre) *On it:* cloth, silver tray, pot of tea,
hot-water jug, jug of milk, sugar, butter, toast rack
with toast, 2 cups, 2 saucers, 2 teaspoons, pot of
marmalade with lid and spoon, 2 small plates, 2
small knives, box with cigarettes and cigarette
holder, table lighter, ashtray, copy of the *Daily
Telegraph*
Upright chair (left of table)
Upright chair (right of table)
Small table (up right centre) *On it:* bowl of flowers
Bookshelves (up left centre) *In them:* books

On them: ashtray,
matches, box with
cigarettes

Personal: **Edward**: nail file
Flora: chiffon handkerchief
Matchseller: balaclava

Offstage: 2 armchairs
Pedlar's tray with boxes of matches (**Matchseller**)
Wicker armchair

During first blackout

Strike:	Table and upright chairs
Set:	*Over terrace:* canopy or awning
	Armchair (left centre)
	Armchair (left)
	On terrace: wicker armchair

LIGHTING PLOT

Property fittings required: none

Interior/Exterior

The main acting areas are the garden and terrace area up centre, the kitchen area right, the breakfast-room area centre and the study area left. These areas are lit independently.

The apparent source of light is daylight

To open: At rise of curtain		(Page 1)
	Bring up lights for bright sunshine effect on garden area up centre and breakfast-room area centre	
Cue 1	Edward: "...other than harmless."	(Page 11)
	Dim all lights to blackout	
Cue 2	When ready	(Page 11)
	Bring up lights on terrace and kitchen area right	
Cue 3	Edward: "Go and get him."	(Page 15)
	Dim out lights on kitchen area right	
Cue 4	Flora: "That's japonica."	(Page 15)
	Bring up lights on study area left	
Cue 5	Edward: "...breath of air."	(Page 21)
	Dim out lights on study area left	
Cue 6	Flora: "...can come in."	(Page 24)
	Bring up lights on study area left	
Cue 7	Flora: "...in the shade."	(Page 24)
	Commence slow dim of general lighting (6 mins)	
Cue 8	Flora: "He's dying."	(Page 26)
	Commence slow dim of general lighting (8 mins)	
Cue 9	At end of Play	(Page 30)
	Dim all lights to blackout	

VISIT THE SAMUEL FRENCH BOOKSHOP AT THE ROYAL COURT THEATRE

Browse plays and theatre books, get expert advice and enjoy a coffee

Samuel French Bookshop
Royal Court Theatre
Sloane Square
London
SW1W 8AS
020 7565 5024

Shop from thousands of titles on our website

 samuelfrench.co.uk

 samuelfrenchltd

 samuel french uk